NUMBER KIT 3

Fair shares

Fractions and decimals

All rights reserved. This book is sold subject to the condition that it shall not, by way of trade or otherwise, be lent, hired out or otherwise circulated without the publisher's prior consent in any form of binding or cover other than that in which it is published and without a similar condition, including this condition, being imposed upon the subsequent purchaser.

No part of this publication may be reproduced, stored in a retrieval system, or transmitted, in any form or by any means, electronic, mechanical, photocopying, recording or otherwise, without the prior permission of the publisher. This book remains copyright, although permission is granted to copy those pages labelled PHOTOCOPIABLE for classroom distribution and use only in the school which has purchased the book, or by the teacher who has purchased this book, and in accordance with the CLA licensing agreement. Photocopying permission is given for purchasers only and not for borrowers of books from any lending service.

British Library Cataloguing-in-Publication Data
A catalogue record for this book is available from the British Library.

ISBN 0-590-53595-1

Published by Scholastic Ltd
Villiers House
Clarendon Avenue
Leamington Spa
Warwickshire CV32 5PR

© 1996 Scholastic Ltd
123456789 6789012345

AUTHOR
Jenny Nash

SERIES CONSULTANT
Sheila Ebbutt
Director of BEAM (Be A Mathematician) which is supported by Islington Council

CURRICULUM LINKS
Ian Gardner, Maths Curriculum Adviser (England and Wales), Megan Emmerson, with Edinburgh Centre for Mathematics Education (Scotland) and Michael Wallace (Northern Ireland)

The publishers wish to thank the following individuals and organisations for their invaluable help in developing the *Maths Focus* concept: Jayne de Courcy, Courcy Consultants; Dr Daphne Kerslake; The Mathematics Centre, Chichester Institute of Higher Education; Oxfordshire Maths Centre; Edinburgh Centre for Mathematics Education; David Bell, Chief Education Officer, City of Newcastle-upon-Tyne; Professor Geoffrey and Dr Julia Matthews.

EDITORIAL TEAM
Irene Goodacre and Libby Weaver

SERIES DESIGNER
Joy White

DESIGNER
Micky Pledge

COVER PHOTOGRAPH
© Bie Bostrom for Scholastic Inc.

ILLUSTRATORS
John Blakeman, Kim Blundell (John Martin & Artists Ltd.), Mik Brown (Kathy Jakeman Illustration), Andy Hamond (Garden Studio), Pat McCarthy, Liz McIntosh (Linda Rogers Associates), Rachael O'Neill (Kathy Jakeman Illustration), Fred Pipes, Jon Riley, William Rudling (John Martin & Artists Ltd)

POSTERMAT
Pat McCarthy

Designed using Aldus Pagemaker
Processed by PAGES Bureau, Leamington Spa
Printed in Great Britain by Ebenezer Baylis & Son, Worcester and George Over, Rugby

© Material from the National Curriculum, Scottish 5–14 Guidelines and the Northern Ireland Curriculum is Crown copyright and is reproduced by permission of the Controller of HMSO, 1995.

CONTENTS

4	WHAT *MATHS FOCUS* OFFERS
6	HERE'S THE MATHS
8	CURRICULUM LINKS
9	USING AND APPLYING GRID

DIAGNOSTIC ASSESSMENT

10	THE SCHOOL FAIR (MONEY)
14	FIND THE FRACTION (FRACTIONS)

ASSESSMENT DOUBLE-CHECK

18	READY FOR SCHOOL (MONEY)
20	FRACTION GRAND PRIX! (FRACTIONS)

REINFORCEMENT ACTIVITIES

22	JIGSAWS
24	THE TIGER WHO STAYED FOR BREAKFAST
26	THREE IN A LINE
28	STACK THE RODS
30	FIRST TO £1
32	MONEY MYSTERIES
34	STAMPS

ENRICHMENT ACTIVITIES

36	GRAB IT!
38	FRACTION NUMBER LINES
40	DESIGN A DECIMAL FRACTION
42	BANK IT!
44	MONEY JOURNEYS

RESOURCES

46	THREE IN A LINE GAME BOARD
47	TRIANGULAR GRID PAPER
48	PHOTOCOPIABLE OF POSTERMAT

MATHS FOCUS

Maths Focus can be used to:

- assess children's knowledge and skills;
- offer reinforcement activities to develop understanding;
- provide enrichment activities to consolidate and extend the learning;
- develop skills and ability in using and applying mathematics.

DIFFERENTIATION

1 *Maths Focus* offers structured progression of content and skills through the Kits 1–5* and provides links with all UK national curricula. With a particular class or year group, you may use activities from more than one kit to cater for all ability levels. Each book focuses on a specific mathematical concept, with activities set in a range of contexts – including games, stories, problems, everyday situations and puzzles – so that children learn to use their mathematics flexibly and appropriately.

2 Assessment activities allow you to evaluate the children's ability to use and apply the mathematics they have learned.

3 Understanding is developed through two types of activity:
- **Reinforcement activities** – which increase children's confidence by concentrating on a specific concept or skill and presenting the maths in a variety of contexts;
- **Enrichment activities** – which consolidate and extend children's learning in more open-ended contexts.

4 Extension ideas at the end of each activity offer ways for more able children to go further in their exploration of a concept.

*See inside back cover for overview of kits and curriculum coverage.

offers...

FLEXIBLE RESOURCE

Maths Focus can be used in a variety of ways to support your teaching of mathematics and your style of teaching, allowing you to use the activities with individuals, groups or the whole class.

Use **Maths Focus** activities alongside a published scheme to:
- develop children's understanding of specific concepts in a greater range of contexts;
- assess children's understanding of a concept, and then to support or extend it with differentiated activities;
- focus on the using and applying aspect of the mathematics curriculum.

If you don't use a published scheme use **Maths Focus**:
- as a core resource when planning your own scheme of work;
- to teach and assess specific concepts.

USING & APPLYING

Aspects of **Using and Applying** covered by each activity are given in the teachers' notes. To help with your planning, the grid on page 9 and the teachers' notes highlight how problem solving, communication and logical reasoning are built into each activity.

USING TALK

All teachers' notes pages offer questions you can ask children to encourage them to talk about what they are doing. Use the questions while they are working to focus their mathematical thinking or at the end of the activity to assess their level of understanding. Most pages also offer:
- **Here's the maths** – explanations of the maths included in the activity;
- **What to look for** – diagnostic pointers to help you to assess whether the child has achieved the mathematical aim of the activity;
- **More help needed** – ways to help children are who struggling with the activity.

ASSESSMENT

Maths Focus offers two types of assessment to be used when you feel appropriate to plan the best way forward for each child.

- You may want to use the **Diagnostic assessment** activity at the start of teaching a concept to establish the existing level of understanding. Alternatively, use it after some initial teaching, to provide a check on progress.

- The **Assessment double-check** allows you to assess the child's understanding of the concept as a whole, to see how their learning has progressed.

RANGE OF RESOURCES

Maths Focus kits come with a full-colour laminated postermat for each book. This flexible wipe-clean resource can be used with a number of the activities in its book and also as a general mathematics resource. Each book has a black and white photocopiable version of its postermat, to use with the activities and for permanent recording of the children's work. Extra postermats are available separately (see inside back cover).

The activities in each book are planned to use a range of mathematical resources, including counting apparatus, number lines and grids and calculators. Mental maths is emphasised throughout.

Both fractions and decimals represent an extension of the children's understanding of the number system. New ideas about decimals are developed through money.

Here's the maths...

Fractions and decimals

What's involved (fractions)

▶ It is important to stress that a fraction, one half for example, can be represented in several ways. The two halves do not need to be identical in shape, only in magnitude (as shown below). In this way **conservation of number** is shown to apply to fractions.

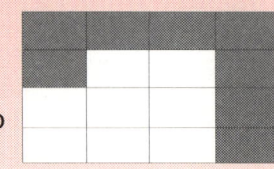

▶ It is also important to stress that a fraction, such as a half, is not an entity in its own right, but relates to a specified whole.

▶ As children encounter fractions in a wider range of contexts they will work with different types:

• a **proper fraction** is one in which the numerator is less than the denominator (such as ¾);

• an **improper fraction** is one in which the numerator is larger than the denominator (such as ³/₂);

• a **mixed number** (such as 1½) is an alternative way of expressing an improper fraction.

▶ Children should be aware that these are all types of **vulgar fraction** and that the word 'decimal' is short for **decimal fraction**.

▶ Vulgar fractions may be thought of as 'unfinished' divisions, while decimal fractions show the division completed. So, for example:

• ½ is one divided by two;
• 0.5 is the result of one divided by two.

CALCULATORS

▶ When using calculators, children need to recognise that many will drop the second decimal place for amounts such as £7.20, where the second digit after the decimal point is a zero, so they will show 7.2. There is a facility on some calculators to 'fix' the number of decimal places to 2.

▶ Calculators provide a useful entry into decimal fractions. Any whole number divided by two, for example, gives either a whole number or a number ending in point five. The magnitude of a decimal number is not necessarily linked to its length, the position of the decimal point being the most important factor.

FAIR SHARES
MATHS FOCUS – NUMBER KIT 3

COMMON MISCONCEPTIONS

◗ Children often make the following mistakes when dealing with fractions:
• 'There are three parts so these must be thirds'
(a fraction is connected to the number of parts a shape is divided into).
• '⁵/₁₀ is greater in magnitude than ½'
(because the digits involved are bigger).
• '1.1976513 is bigger than 2'
(because it has more digits).
• When a unit is sub-divided the pieces must be the same size and shape in order to be the same fraction.

What's involved (decimals and money)

◗ Work on decimals should arise from meaningful contexts, particularly money. Strictly speaking £1.50 is not the same as 1.5 but through working with money you can encourage connections such as: 50p = £0.50 = ½, 0.5 or ⁵/₁₀ of a pound.

◗ As well as the notion of a fraction within a unit, work on sequences can help children to identify decimals as points along a number line:

◗ As children are introduced to decimal fractions they will begin to recognise common quantities within a unit such as 0.5 or 0.75.

◗ The use of decimals greatly simplifies the introduction of operations like addition on vulgar fractions. However, not all fractions can be expressed *exactly* as decimal fractions (for example ¹/₃, which is 0.333, where the 3 is repeated continually).

◗ Once they recognise common decimal fractions, such as 0.5 or 0.25, children will begin to order other quantities through comparison.

WORKING WITH MONEY

◗ It is not necessary to have a full understanding of the place value nature of the digits when recording quantities of pounds and pence such as £1.26.

◗ It is important to work in real and imaginary contexts, but always using real coins as:
• plastic or card coins are usually unrealistic;
• new denominations of coins are introduced, and the size and shape of existing coins are sometimes changed.

◗ Denominations of coins, although not arbitrary, are not directly linked to the place value system of multiples of 10. Children must therefore be competent in counting on in 2s, 5s, 10s and 20s from any given number. Developing these skills will support effective strategies for giving and receiving change in money situations.

KEY FACTS

• The usual way of denoting fractions is to place below the line the number of equal parts into which the unit is divided (denominator) and above the line the number of these parts comprising the fraction (numerator).
• Children should become aware of the inter-relatedness and equivalence of common fractions, decimals and percentages, for example 0.5 = ½ = 50%.

KEY WORDS

decimal point
fraction
whole unit
multiple
factor
part
equivalent
numerator
denominator

FAIR SHARES
MATHS FOCUS – NUMBER KIT 3

Curriculum links

This chart outlines the particular strands and statements from each of the UK curriculum documents for maths that apply to the content of this book.

The processes outlined opposite show how this maths is applied to a range of contexts and how outcomes are reported.

MATHEMATICS IN THE NATIONAL CURRICULUM (ENGLAND AND WALES)

This book covers the following statements from the Key Stage 2 Programme of Study for Number:

▶ Pupils should be given opportunities to:
• develop flexible and effective methods of computation and recording, and use them with understanding;
• use calculators ... as tools for exploring number structure and to enable work with realistic data;
• develop the skills needed for accurate and appropriate use of equipment. (1a, b [part], c)
  Pupils should be taught to:
▶ Develop an understanding of place value and extend the number system;
• extend their understanding of the number system to ... decimals with no more than two decimal places in the context of ... money;
• understand and use, in context, fractions ... to describe and compare proportions of a whole. (2b [part], c [part])
▶ Understand relationships between numbers and develop methods of computation
• extend methods of computation to include addition and subtraction with ... all four operations with decimals, and calculating fractions ... of quantities, using a calculator where appropriate. (3g [part])
▶ Solve numerical problems
• develop their use of the four operations to solve problems, including those involving money and measures, using a calculator where appropriate;
• choose sequences of methods of computation appropriate to a problem, adapt them and apply them accurately;
• check results by different methods, including repeating the operations in a different order or using inverse operations; gain a sense of the size of a solution and estimate and approximate solutions to problems. (4a, b, c)
Since this book is relevant to the middle primary years, the activities may be found to overlap between the above Key Stage 2 areas and similar areas at Key Stage 1.

MATHEMATICS 5–14 (SCOTTISH GUIDELINES)

This book covers the following strands of the Attainment Outcome Number, Money and Measurement
▶ Money
• **Work with**: whole numbers up to 100 and then up to 1000 (count, order, read/write). (Level B)
▶ Range and type of numbers:
• **Work with**: thirds, fifths, eighths, tenths and simple equivalences such as one half = two quarters (practical applications only). (Level C)

NORTHERN IRELAND CURRICULUM FOR MATHEMATICS

This book covers these strands of Number from the Programme of Study for mathematics at Key Stage 1:
▶ Understanding number and number notation
Pupils should have opportunities to:
(d) recognise and use simple everyday fractions and their notation in practical situations.
▶ Money
(a) recognise and know how to use coins in simple contexts...; use and understand the conventional way of recording in money...; use these skills in problem-solving situations.

8 FAIR SHARES
MATHS FOCUS – NUMBER KIT 3

Using and applying

All of the activities in Maths Focus involve applying mathematics in specific context. This chart will help you to identify the particular strands of Using and Applying Mathematics that are part of each activity. Problem-solving and Enquiry (Scottish 5–14 Guidelines) and Processes (NI Curriculum) are also addressed through these statements.

Activities	Problem Solving	Communication	Logical Reasoning
DIAGNOSTIC ASSESSMENT			
The school fair	Find alternative solutions.	Explain the reason for the choice of coins. Record results.	
Find the fraction	Find different ways of representing the same fractions.	Explain choices.	Understand why two fractions might be equivalent.
ASSESSMENT DOUBLE-CHECK			
Ready for school	Select a calculator (or other resource) to complete the task.	Present calculations pictorially, in words or in figures.	Use trial and improvement methods.
Fraction Grand Prix!	Select an effective mental strategy for calculating dice differences.	Use appropriate vocabulary when moving along the track.	Predict landing squares using mental calculation and without first moving the counter.
REINFORCEMENT ACTIVITIES			
Jigsaws	Decide how to plan and organise work to solve a problem.		Show the ability to reach conclusions by connecting facts and ideas from previous experience.
The Tiger who stayed for breakfast	Attempt a complex task in a familiar context. Decide how to use equipment to solve problems.	Use the language of fractions.	
Three in a line	Check results by deciding if the answer is reasonable, using a range of methods.	Work well with others.	Make guesses and test them out, accepting the results of the test. Show the ability to reach conclusions by connecting ideas and facts from previous experience.
Stack the rods	Plan a suitable sequence of work for a set task.	Show knowledge of the systematic structure of the number system through developing ideas of equivalence. Use the language of equivalent fractions. Interpret own recording.	
First to £1			Respond to 'What if…' questions.
Money mysteries		Discuss simple calculations which involve money. Use appropriate language connected with money.	Solve a problem by seeking relevant information.
Stamps	Decide how to use money to solve problems.	Invent simple ways of recording.	
ENRICHMENT ACTIVITIES			
Grab it!		Develop the ability to work with others.	
Fraction number lines	Show perseverance and overcome difficulties.	Read and write fractions. Show knowledge of the structure of the number system.	
Design a decimal fraction	Decide how to plan and organise a problem. Plan a suitable sequence of work for a set task.		
Bank it!	Check results (decide if the amount of coins counted out is correct).		Connect facts and ideas learned from working with small amounts of money to using larger amounts.
Money journeys		Explain the work being done, including processes and difficulties.	Show the ability to reach conclusions by connecting facts and ideas from previous experience.

FAIR SHARES
MATHS FOCUS – NUMBER KIT 3

TALK ABOUT

- *'Could you pay that amount using fewer coins?'*
- *'How did you work out which coins to use?'*
- *'Can you explain how you recorded your working?'*
- *'Are there any other ways of making the same amount?'*
- *'Can you show a different way of writing that amount using a pound sign?'*

DIAGNOSTIC ASSESSMENT (MONEY)

The school fair

Key aims
- To discover how confident the child is about:
- using combinations of coins to £1;
- using decimal notation in recording money.

What you need
- a bank of coins
- pencils
- 1 copy of each activity sheet for each child

Organisation
- Children should work in groups of four. Assess individuals by observing closely.

The activity
- Give each child a copy of the two photocopiable pages.
- Explain that they have been given some money to spend at the school fair. The stalls don't have much change, so they need to pay the right amount of money if they can.
- They should try to find two different ways of making up each amount using coins.
- They then record the value of the coins they used on the second sheet.
- Encourage the children to select the coins they will use before writing down their values.
- You can alter the amounts they must pay before photocopying the sheets to suit different ability levels.

Where next?
- Challenge the children to pay each amount using the smallest possible number of coins.

Name _____

The school fair

ASSESSING
USING & APPLYING

PROBLEM SOLVING
▶ Find alternative solutions.

COMMUNICATION
▶ Explain the reason for the choice of coins.
▶ Record results.

DIAGNOSTIC ASSESSMENT (MONEY)

Assessing understanding

▶ Look for the following to indicate that the children are ready for **Enrichment activities**. They may:
- be able to identify the coins needed to make the stated amounts;
- be able to find a way of showing which coins they chose to use;
- be able to record the amounts using decimal notation, for example £0.53;
- discuss the reasons for their choices confidently, for example, '53p... I used 50p, 2p, and 1p because that's just three coins... I could have used two twenties and a ten instead of the 50.'

▶ Look for the following to indicate that the children are in need of further work on the concept of money. They may:
- be unable to explain or discuss the reasons for their choices;
- be unable to find coins for most or all of the amounts on the activity sheet;
- be unable to use some of the larger value coins, relying instead upon the smaller ones;
- be unable to record using decimal notation correctly.

Children who need more help

▶ Children who lack confidence, cannot find coins for amounts on the activity sheet, or are unable to use some of the coins, need more experience of counting out with coins. Go on to the **Reinforcement activities** 'First to £1' (page 30) or 'Money mysteries' (page 32).

▶ Children who cannot explain their methods or talk about coins should be given more opportunities to link practical work and discussion. Try the **Reinforcement activities** 'Money mysteries' (page 32) or 'Stamps' (page 34).

▶ Children who are unable to write amounts using decimal notation will probably need specific experience of relating amounts of money to written symbols. Go on to the **Reinforcement activity** 'First to £1' (page 30).

FAIR SHARES
MATHS FOCUS – NUMBER KIT 3

Name _____

The school fair

You have saved some money to spend at the School Fair.
Choose four items. **Find** two ways to pay for each.

I bought

I used

I used

I bought

I used

I used

I bought

I used

I used

I bought

I used

I used

PHOTOCOPIABLE

FAIR SHARES

TALK ABOUT

- 'How did you decide that this picture shows a third?'
- 'What would two quarters look like?'
- 'How else could you show that fraction?'
- 'Can you find $1/3$ of 6?'
- 'Which is bigger: $1/2$ or $1/3$?'
- 'Why do we write fractions like this?'

DIAGNOSTIC ASSESSMENT (FRACTIONS)

Find the fraction

Key aim
- To discover how confident the child is about identifying and finding fractions of objects, sets and numbers.

What you need
- pencils
- 1 copy of each activity sheet for each child
- sheets of paper cut into different shapes: rectangles, circles, ovals and squares

Organisation
- The children could work in a group of four while you act as an observer to assess them individually.

The activity
- Give each child a cut-out sheet of paper and ask them to fold it into equal fractions – halves or quarters or thirds. They should then write the fraction in each folded section of the whole:

$\frac{1}{4}$	$\frac{1}{4}$	$\frac{1}{4}$	$\frac{1}{4}$

- Observe what they do, then give each child a copy of the photocopiable page.
- Discuss the sheet and remind the children that equal fractions are equal parts of a whole. Leave them to work independently.
- Children who complete the first sheet without difficulty should try splitting the grids on the second sheet to make quarters. This part of the activity could be introduced by letting the children use LEGO bricks to build and split walls.

Where next?
- The children can try to find as many ways as they can of showing halves and quarters, perhaps making a 'half-sized' poster and a 'quarter-sized' poster.

FAIR SHARES
MATHS FOCUS – NUMBER KIT 3

Name _____

Find the fraction

These pictures all show fractions.
They show either $\frac{1}{2}$ or $\frac{1}{3}$ or $\frac{1}{4}$.
Write the fraction next to the picture.

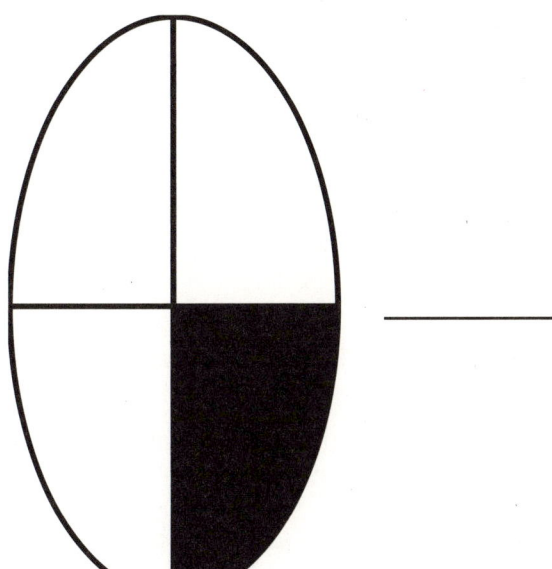 ____

 ____

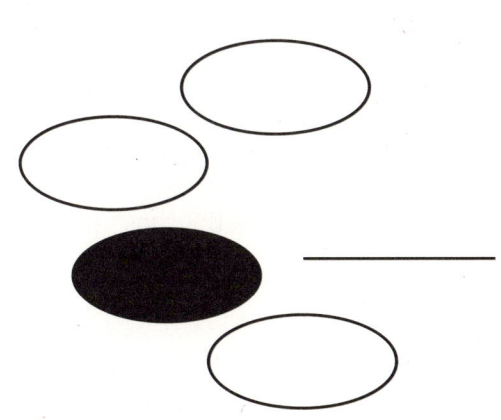 ____

____

Has this shape been split into

halves? _____

How do you know? _____

ASSESSING USING & APPLYING

PROBLEM SOLVING
◗ Find different ways of representing the same fractions.
COMMUNICATION
◗ Explain choices.
LOGICAL REASONING
◗ Understand why two fractions might be equivalent.

DIAGNOSTIC ASSESSMENT (FRACTIONS)

Assessing understanding

◗ Look for the following to indicate that the children are ready for **Enrichment activities**. They may:
- be able to identify and find fractions of objects confidently;
- be able to explain the reasons for their decisions;
- demonstrate that they understand equivalence when quartering the rectangles;
- find fractions of sets, possibly using objects to help them.

◗ Look for the following to indicate that the children need further work on the concept of fractions. They may:
- think that a shape cut in two has been halved regardless of the size of the pieces;
- be unable to explain or discuss the reasons for their decisions;
- be unable to identify or find fractions of objects or sets;
- have difficulty in thinking of different ways of quartering rectangles.

Children who need more help

◗ Children who lack confidence, are unable to talk about fractions or show poor understanding of fractions of objects need more experience of cutting shapes and related discussion. Try the **Reinforcement activity** 'Jigsaws' (page 22).

◗ Those who cannot find fractions of sets of objects will benefit from work on splitting sets. Try the **Reinforcement activity** 'The Tiger who stayed for breakfast' (page 24).

◗ Children who are unable to find fractions of numbers will benefit from the further practice provided by the **Reinforcement activity** 'Three in a line' (page 26).

◗ Those who demonstrate a lack of understanding of equivalence need practical activities to help develop their mental image of fractions and how they relate to one another. Go on to the **Reinforcement activity** 'Stack the rods' (page 28).

Name _____

Find the fraction

Divide these rectangles into quarters in different ways.
You could colour them or cut them into pieces.

PHOTOCOPIABLE

FAIR SHARES
MATHS FOCUS – NUMBER KIT 3

17

ASSESSMENT DOUBLE-CHECK (MONEY)

Ready for school

Key aims
▶ To discover how confident the child is about:
• solving problems involving money;
• recording using decimal notation.

What you need
▶ 1 activity sheet per child
▶ pencils and paper
▶ calculators

Organisation
▶ Children can collaborate on this or they may complete the task independently. If the children work in groups you will need to observe closely to assess individuals' level of understanding.

Introduction
▶ Tell the children they must solve three problems.
▶ Read through the worksheet together and explain that calculators are available if they need them.

The activity
▶ Give a copy of the activity sheet to each child.
▶ Explain that the second and third questions rely on trial and improvement and reassure them that they may need to have a few attempts before they get the right answers.
▶ Leave them to work independently.

Assessing understanding
▶ Look for:
• confidence in handling the two different notations presented on the activity sheet (pence only and pounds/pence);
• an ability to combine amounts of money;
• perseverance in trying possible combinations.

Children who need more help
▶ If children have difficulty with the relative open-endedness of the second and third questions these could be replaced with some direct and closed questions, perhaps in a form such as: pencils and ruler → total ☐
▶ Check that children know how to enter the figures into the calculator with regard for the decimal point and place value.

ASSESSING USING & APPLYING

PROBLEM SOLVING
▶ Does the child select a calculator (or other resource) to complete the task?

COMMUNICATION
▶ Can the child present calculations pictorially, in words or in figures?

LOGICAL REASONING
▶ Does the child use trial and improvement methods?

TALK ABOUT

For the first question:
▶ 'How do you write that amount in figures?'

For the second question:
▶ 'How much more do you need to make that total?'

For the third question:
▶ 'Could you try a different combination?'

FAIR SHARES
MATHS FOCUS – NUMBER KIT 3

Name _____

Ready for school

- How much would these items cost in total?
- How could you spend exactly £2 on three of these items?
- If you spend £2.90 on pencil cases and felt-tips, how many of each would you get?

PHOTOCOPIABLE

ASSESSMENT DOUBLE-CHECK (FRACTIONS)

Fraction Grand Prix!

Key aims
▶ To discover how confident the child is about:
• calculating simple differences between fractions;
• matching conventional fractions to their decimal equivalents;
• counting on along a fraction number line.

What you need
▶ 1 activity sheet for each pair
▶ counters (or car cut-outs)
▶ two dice (both labelled 0, ½, 1, 1½, 2, 2½)

Organisation
▶ Children could be paired by friendship or ability.

Introduction
▶ This assessment can be carried out while children are playing the game. You may need to talk to some children individually to confirm their understanding.

The activity
▶ Give one activity sheet to each pair and a different coloured counter to each child.
▶ Explain the rules:
• Place your counters on zero.
• Take turns to roll the dice.
• Calculate the difference between the two fractions.
• Use your result to move forward along the fraction number line.
• The winner is the first player to finish.

Assessing understanding
▶ Look for:
• confidence in manipulating the fractions on the dice;
• an understanding of counting on in halves along the number line;
• an ability to predict the landing space before moving the counter.

Children who need more help
▶ If children have difficulty calculating the dice differences, play the game with one dice only. Players move the amount shown on the dice.

ASSESSING USING & APPLYING

PROBLEM SOLVING
▶ Does the child select an effective mental strategy for calculating dice differences?

COMMUNICATION
▶ Does the child use appropriate vocabulary when moving along the track?

LOGICAL REASONING
▶ Can the child predict landing squares using mental calculation and without first moving the counter?

TALK ABOUT
▶ 'What is the difference this time?'
▶ 'How did you work it out?'
▶ 'Where will that score take you?'
▶ 'How much more do you need to win?'

Name _____

Fraction Grand Prix!

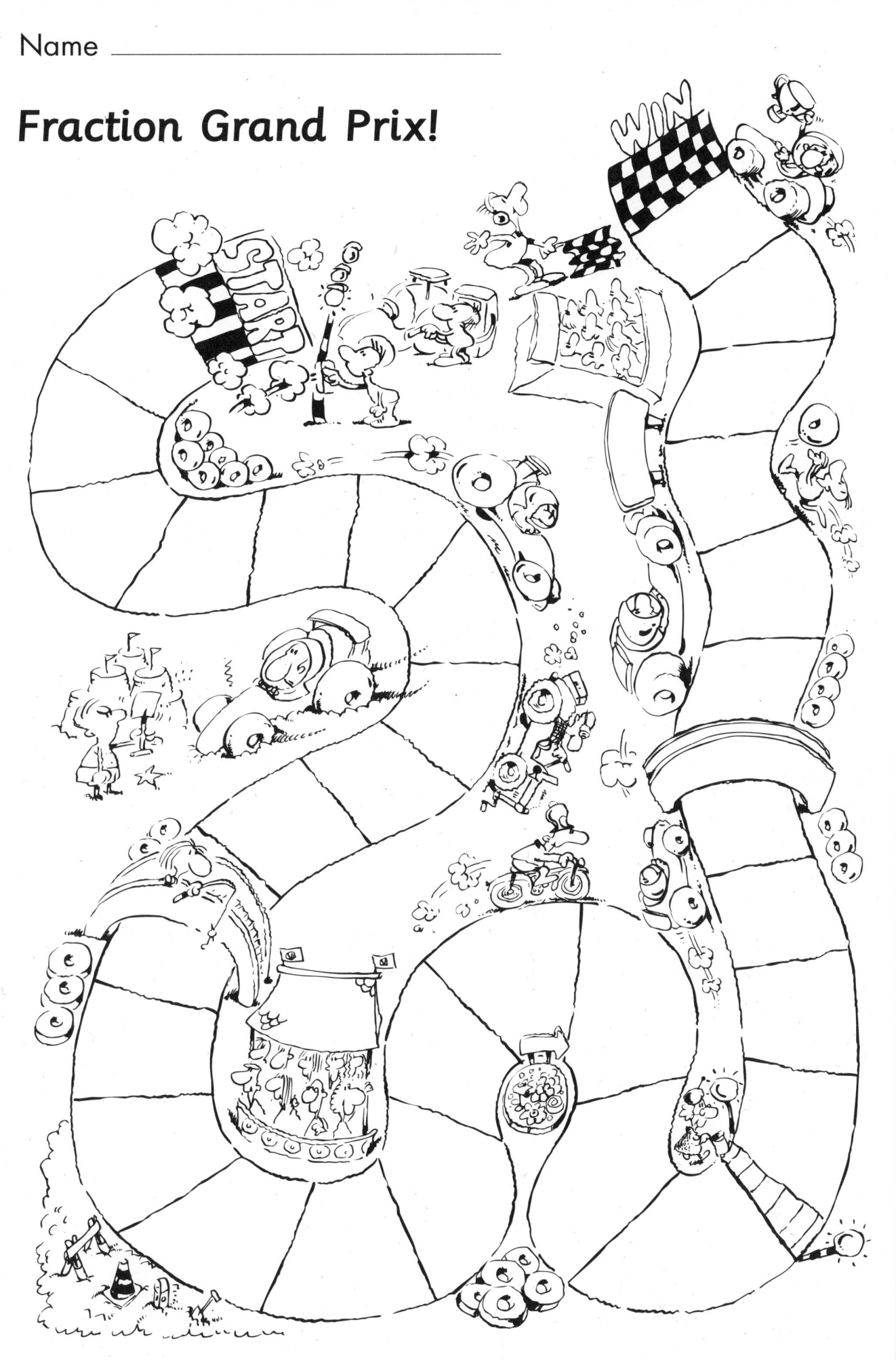

PHOTOCOPIABLE

REINFORCEMENT ACTIVITY

Jigsaws

Key aim
◗ To develop understanding of fractions of objects and quantities.

What you need
◗ several copies of the activity sheet for each child
◗ scissors
◗ colouring pencils or crayons
◗ scrap paper

The activity
◗ Demonstrate how to make a fraction jigsaw by cutting one of the grids into quarters so that each piece is a different shape, but has the same number of whole squares.
◗ Encourage the children to divide the 16-square grid into quarters.
◗ Remind them that each quarter must be a different shape.
◗ They can then cut out their pieces and ask a friend to reassemble the quarters into a complete grid.
◗ Children could go on to divide the grids into eighths, using the same rules.

Extension ideas
◗ Challenge the children to find fifths or tenths of any of the grids on the activity sheet.
◗ Let the children use the scrap paper to draw out their own grids and make up fraction jigsaws with different pieces.

USING & APPLYING

PROBLEM SOLVING
◗ Decide how to plan and organise work to solve a problem.
LOGICAL REASONING
◗ Show the ability to reach conclusions by connecting facts and ideas from previous experience.

TALK ABOUT
◗ 'How many squares are there in the whole grid?'
◗ 'How many squares are there in a quarter of this grid?'
◗ 'Can you explain why both these pieces are a quarter when they have such different shapes?'
◗ 'Can you think of any other fractions we could divide this grid up into?'

HERE'S THE MATHS
◗ This activity involves the idea of different shapes having the same area and so representing the same fraction of the whole grid.

WHAT TO LOOK FOR
◗ Are all four pieces a different shape? Are they all the same size? Do the children realise that pieces can have the same area, but a different shape?

MORE HELP NEEDED
◗ A 'half' jigsaw could be used.

FAIR SHARES

Jigsaws

Make a Quarters Jigsaw.

Cut up the first grid into four pieces. See if you can make each piece a different shape. Each piece must have the same number of squares in it.

Give your Jigsaw to someone to fit together again.

Make some different Quarters Jigsaws from the other grids.

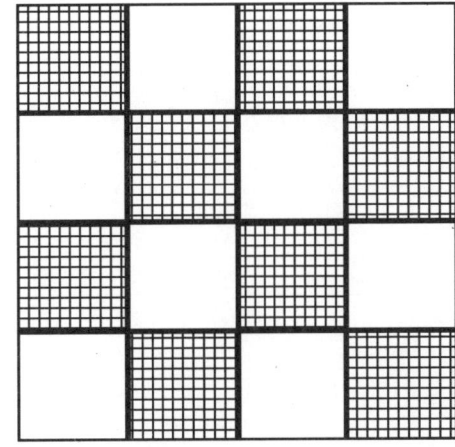
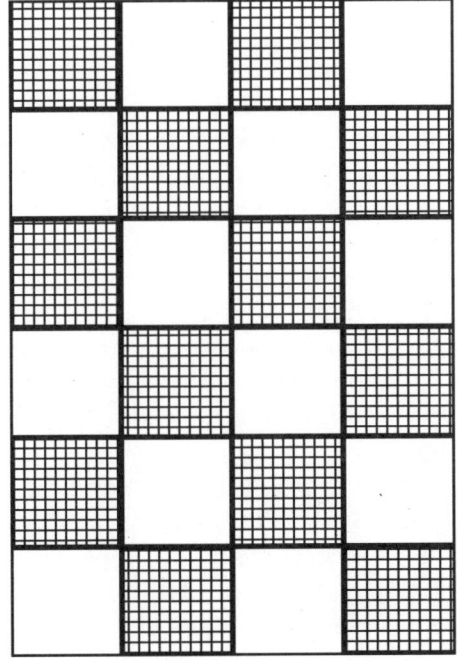
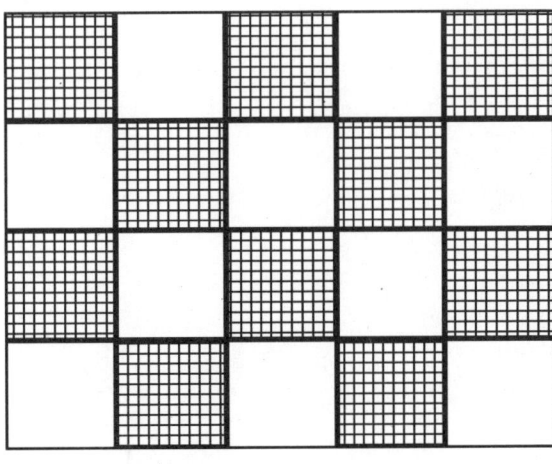
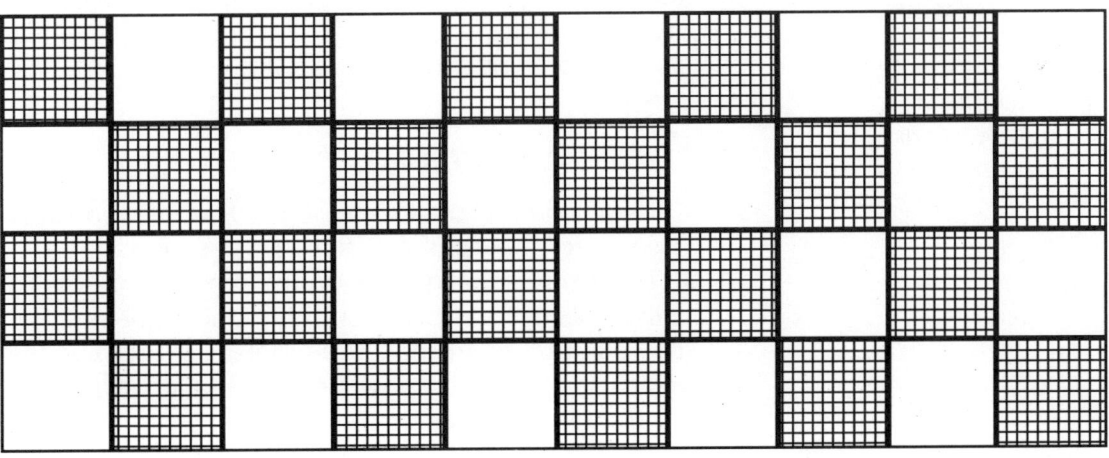

PHOTOCOPIABLE

FAIR SHARES

USING & APPLYING

PROBLEM SOLVING
- Attempt a complex task in a familiar context.
- Decide how to use equipment to solve problems.

COMMUNICATION
- Use the language of fractions.

TALK ABOUT

- 'How did you work that out?'
- 'Can you find a different fraction of the set of toast?'
- 'Which fraction so far has given you the most pieces of toast?'
- 'Can you explain what you have learned today?'

HERE'S THE MATHS

- Working out fractions of a number of items is an important feature of the understanding of fractions.
- It is also a natural development of the 'sharing' aspect of division. If 12 pieces of toast are shared between three children, each gets $1/3$ of the toast pieces.

WHAT TO LOOK FOR

- Can the children demonstrate how they carried out the task?

MORE HELP NEEDED

- Use this as a sharing activity and emphasise the language of fractions at the same time.

REINFORCEMENT ACTIVITY

The Tiger who stayed for breakfast

Key aims
- To provide practice in finding fractions of sets and numbers.
- To use the conventions of recording fractions.

What you need
- *The Tiger who came to tea* by Judith Kerr (Picture Lions)
- counters, cubes, number lines
- 1 activity sheet for each child
- scissors, paper and pencils

The activity
- Seat the children in a group so that they can all see the pictures in the book as you read it to them.
- Read *The Tiger who came to tea* or, if the book is not available, tell the story of a tiger who came to tea with a little girl called Sophie, and ate and drank everything in the house, including all the water in the taps!
- Stop at appropriate points in the story and discuss, for example, how many buns might have been on the plate and how many would be left if the tiger only ate half of them. You could use apparatus to help solve these problems.
- Demonstrate how to find half of a number using a number line and a fraction of a set of objects.
- Remind the children that the bottom (the denominator) of a fraction tells you how many parts the whole set is divided into and the top (the numerator) how many of those parts are to be shown. Practise finding fractions of sets of objects.
- Introduce the activity sheet and ask the children what they think would have happened if the tiger had come back the next morning for breakfast (after Sophie and her Mummy had been shopping). Talk through the questions, then leave the children to work on the task.

Extension ideas
- The children could create other breakfast problems with boiled eggs, bowls of cereal, or glasses of orange juice.
- The children could work on the problem of how to share two pieces of toast between three children. Ask them what they might need to solve the problem. If they suggest using bread, and this is not possible, they could use pieces of paper cut to represent the toast.

The Tiger who stayed for breakfast

There were 12 pieces of toast in the rack before the tiger came along.

How many pieces of toast would the tiger have if he ate $\frac{1}{4}$ of the toast?

Work it out and complete the number sentence...

$\frac{1}{4}$ of 12 = _____

How many pieces would the tiger have if he ate $\frac{1}{3}$ of the toast?

$\frac{1}{3}$ of 12 = _____

How many pieces would the tiger have if he only ate $\frac{1}{6}$ of the toast?

$\frac{1}{6}$ of 12 = _____

What if there were 16 pieces of toast in the rack instead?

$\frac{1}{2}$ of 16 = _____

Find more fractions of 16 and write your own number sentences like those above.

PHOTOCOPIABLE

USING & APPLYING

PROBLEM SOLVING
◗ Check results by deciding if the answer is reasonable, using a range of methods.
COMMUNICATION
◗ Work well with others.
LOGICAL REASONING
◗ Make guesses and test them out, accepting the results of the test.
◗ Show the ability to reach conclusions by connecting ideas and facts from previous experience.

TALK ABOUT

◗ 'How did you work it out?'
◗ 'Could you think of another way to work it out?'
◗ 'Can you see another way to make that number?'
◗ 'Why is half of this number more that half of this one?'
◗ 'Could you try to work out the next one in your head?'

HERE'S THE MATHS

◗ Games provide a useful way of practising skills. Here the children develop flexibility in calculating fractions of a whole number. The division aspect of a fraction, which the calculator emphasises, is very important.

WHAT TO LOOK FOR

◗ Do the children know which fractions of numbers can be worked out to give a whole number and which won't?

MORE HELP NEEDED

◗ Ensure that all the fractions relate to countable objects, rather than to abstract numbers.

REINFORCEMENT ACTIVITY

Three in a line

Key aims
◗ To consolidate the use of counting apparatus to find fractions of numbers.
◗ To develop the ability to find fractions of numbers using mental methods.
◗ To introduce the use of calculators to find fractions of numbers.
◗ To show that the size of a fraction is dependent upon the size of the whole of which it is a part.

What you need
◗ counters (or small cubes) in two colours
◗ counting apparatus (conkers, links and so on)
◗ 1 activity sheet and 1 game board (photocopiable page 46) between two
◗ pencils and plain paper
◗ calculators

Organisation
◗ This game is played in pairs.
◗ Have all the equipment ready to hand and make sure that there are sufficient quantities of counters in two colours.
◗ Group the children round the photocopiable page.

The activity
◗ Ask two children to demonstrate the game. They should both take turns until you are sure that everyone watching is clear about how to play.
◗ Remind the group that winning lines can be diagonal as well as vertical or horizontal, and that some numbers can be made in different ways: so 2 is $\frac{1}{2}$ of 4 but also $\frac{1}{3}$ of 6.
◗ Show how the calculator can be used to find a fraction: such as $\frac{1}{2}$ of 8 is 8 ÷ 2.
◗ Encourage the children to come up with methods to check their answers.

Extension ideas
◗ Ask the children to record all the number sentences it is possible to make using the fractions and numbers on the board: $\frac{1}{3}$ of 9 is 3, $\frac{1}{2}$ of 10 is 5 and so on.
◗ Encourage the children to devise their own games for others to play.

FAIR SHARES

Three in a line

The aim of this game is to be the first player to cover three squares in a line.

The line can be horizontal ●●●

or vertical

or diagonal

- Each player takes counters of one colour.
- Decide who will play first.
- Choose a fraction from the sun and a number from the cloud to make a question, then say it out loud like this: '$\frac{1}{2}$ of 30?'
- Select the square which you think shows the answer.
- Both players together then find a way to check if the answer is right.
- If the answer is correct you can put your counter on the square. If it's wrong you can't!
- Now the second player has a go.

Take it in turns until someone has three counters in a line.

REINFORCEMENT ACTIVITY

Stack the rods

Key aims
◗ To develop understanding of the equivalence of fractions of a whole through practical activity.

What you need
◗ coloured rods
◗ plain and colouring pencils
◗ 1 activity sheet for each child

The activity
◗ This activity involves using coloured rods to build walls. The children may need some time to experiment with the rods if they have not worked with them for a while.
◗ Encourage them to notice the relationships between the rods, for example 'four of this colour are the same length as two of that colour'.
◗ Ask the children to select an eight rod and build on top of it; remind them that the rods in each layer should be equal in length.
◗ Once they have found all the possible equivalent fractions for this rod ask them to record the equivalent fractions they have found on the activity sheet.
◗ Encourage the children to say the fraction aloud:
• 'One green is $1/3$ of the black and green'.
• 'One green is $1/2$ of a black'.

Extension ideas
◗ The children can generate equivalent fractions by folding paper. Ask them to halve a piece of paper and, keeping it folded, halve it again…and again. They then open it up and identify equivalent fractions by looking at the folded sections.

USING & APPLYING

PROBLEM SOLVING
◗ Plan a suitable sequence of work for a set task.

COMMUNICATION
◗ Show knowledge of the systematic structure of the number system through developing ideas of equivalence.
◗ Use the language of equivalent fractions.
◗ Interpret own recording.

TALK ABOUT

◗ 'Can you find a different rod that will fit along the long one?'
◗ 'How can you write down what you have found out?'
◗ 'Can you tell me what an equivalent fraction is?'

HERE'S THE MATHS

◗ The process of finding rods of the same colour to make a given length can be done by trial and error or, if children are aware of the numerical values, can be calculated by knowing about fractions. Having found, for example, four blue rods to make a given rod, the language of fractions is appropriate and the idea of equivalence follows for finding other ways of representing the same length.

WHAT TO LOOK FOR

◗ Do the children use rods of the same colour for the layer of the wall?
◗ Do they identify the appropriate fraction?
◗ Do they realise that only certain colours will work for a given total length?

FAIR SHARES
MATHS FOCUS – NUMBER KIT 3

Name _____

Stack the rods

Use coloured rods to find equivalent fractions by building fraction walls.

Take a long rod and build up as many as possible on top, like this:

Now make some fraction walls of your own – record these below.

PHOTOCOPIABLE

FAIR SHARES

REINFORCEMENT ACTIVITY

First to £1

Key aims
◗ To develop familiarity with money to £1.
◗ To practise exchanging coins in the context of a game.
◗ To provide practice in totalling amounts using a calculator.

What you need
◗ 1 copy of the activity sheet for each child
◗ a bank of coins
◗ a blank dice marked 1p 2p 5p 10p, with two blanks
◗ calculators, spare sheets of paper.

Organisation
◗ Prepare the dice by marking the faces 1p, 2p, 5p, 10p.
◗ This game is best played in groups of three or four.

The activity
◗ Hand out the activity sheets, then gather the children around while you demonstrate the game.
◗ Explain that each child should draw something in which money is kept in the bottom half of their activity sheet – this is the 'safe area'. They can choose what they want to draw – perhaps a purse, a bank, a wallet, a money box, or a sack.
◗ Ask two children to demonstrate the game.
◗ Explain that they take turns to throw the dice but that this game is unusual because each player can **choose** how many times he throws the dice in one turn.
◗ The player who throws the dice can collect coins to the value shown, keeping the money in the top half of the page. If a blank is thrown, then the player loses all the money won during that turn.
◗ When the player decides to stop throwing the dice the money can be put into the safe area in the bottom half of the page and cannot then be lost in subsequent turns.
◗ Ask the children to use calculators to keep running totals (on a separate sheet of paper) of the money in their safe area. The first person to collect £1 (or over) in a safe area wins.
◗ When the game is over let the children exchange their coins so that they have the smallest possible number of coins.

Extension ideas
◗ Make a dice with different coin values on the faces, say 5p, 10p, 20p, 50p and change the winning total to £5.00.
◗ Change the dice so that there is one more blank face. The children can discuss their strategy for the game before starting and then again afterwards.

USING & APPLYING

LOGICAL REASONING
◗ Respond to 'What if...' questions.

◗ 'How many throws are you going to take this time? Why?'
◗ 'How much money have you got so far?'
◗ 'Can you see anyone who has more/less money than you?'
◗ 'Can you think of a way of improving your chances of winning more money?'

TALK ABOUT

HERE'S THE MATHS
◗ This activity involves the idea of probability as the children have to decide when to end their turn. The need to keep a running total, to know who wins, will encourage mental addition.

MORE HELP NEEDED
◗ Give the children a smaller total to reach.

---

30 FAIR SHARES
MATHS FOCUS – NUMBER KIT 3

Name _____

First to £1

Draw something on your paper that you can keep your money in. This is your safe area.

Take turns to throw the money dice.

- You can have as many throws as you like, but your turn is over if you throw a blank before you decide to stop.
- If you throw a blank you lose the money you have won in that turn.
- If you stop your turn before you throw a blank you put your money in the safe area.

Use a calculator to keep track of how much money you have in your safe area.

The first person to have £1 in their safe area is the winner.

REINFORCEMENT ACTIVITY

Money mysteries

Key aims
- To use knowledge of coin value to solve problems.
- To develop flexible mental calculations with money.

What you need
- a bank of coins
- 1 copy of the activity sheet between two

Organisation
- Ensure that there are enough coins for the groups to work on the activity.

The activity
- Tell children that they will be making and solving their own money mysteries.
- Start by presenting the children with your own money mystery, guiding them towards solving it.
  - 'I have a total of 12 pence.'
  - 'I have four coins.'
  - 'Which coins do I have?'
- Ask each child, in turn, to make up another money mystery.
- Suggest that they use a small number of coins to start with, and that the first clue they give is the total value of their coins. Encourage them to use the coins on the table to try to solve each other's mysteries. When you are sure that they are capable of giving useful clues let them move on to the activity sheet, working in pairs.

Extension ideas
- Encourage the children to increase the complexity of their clues:
  - 'No two coins are alike.'
  - 'All the coins are round.'
  - 'The amount is between 10p and 20p.'
- Make a money mysteries book with a different mystery on each page.

USING & APPLYING

COMMUNICATION
- Discuss simple calculations which involve money.
- Use appropriate language connected with money.

LOGICAL REASONING
- Solve a problem by seeking relevant information.

TALK ABOUT
- 'Try four 5p coins. Is the total too high or too low?'
- 'What will you try next? Is that too high or too low?'
- 'Which coins will you have to change?'
- 'Why is it that some mysteries have more than one answer?'

HERE'S THE MATHS
- Children need practice in calculating amounts of money in their heads.
- By having to ask questions they need to decide what information is useful.

WHAT TO LOOK FOR
- Do the children ask useful questions?
- Do they elicit new information with each question?

Name _____

Solve the money mystery

These dogs all have coins in their hands. One is holding 17p. Can you tell which one?

Which coins does that dog have? _____

Make your own money mystery.
Work with a partner.
Take some coins, but don't tell what coins you took.
Give some clues.
Say how much money you have.
Say how many coins you have.

Your partner must **guess** which coins you have in your hand.
Think up more money mysteries.
Make up different clues.

REINFORCEMENT ACTIVITY

Stamps

Key aims
◗ To solve problems using money.
◗ To relate coin values to amounts of money.
◗ To encourage flexibility in mental calculations.

What you need
◗ a bank of coins
◗ a good supply of scissors
◗ plain paper, pencils, glue
◗ 1 copy of the activity sheet for each child

Introduction
◗ This activity is very open ended. Be prepared for the children to suggest their own avenues for investigation; if this happens you will need to make a judgement about whether to explore these at the time or come back to them later.

The activity
◗ Give each child a stamp sheet and explain that they are going to make their own stamps.
◗ Tell them that they can make two rows of 3p stamps and two rows of 5p stamps, but that they will need to write the value of each stamp in the appropriate place.
◗ Ask them to colour these stamps and cut them out.
◗ When they have finished this task, ask if they can see a way to put stamps worth 15p on a letter.
◗ Encourage them to use their stamps and calculate mentally.
◗ When you have a variety of solutions ask them to show you which coins they could use to pay for the stamps.
◗ Ask the children to find out which amounts from 1p up to 50p they can make with their stamps and show how they would pay for them.
◗ Encourage them to find their own way of recording.

Extension ideas
◗ Challenge the children to cover every value up to 50p using two, or possibly three, values of stamp. Set a limit on the number of stamps which can be used to make up an amount.
◗ The children could work on a related activity using stamps of different values.
◗ They could make envelopes, stick stamps on them and 'sell' them to each other using coins.
◗ They could try to work on amounts up to £1; this will take some time and is best done as a group, pooling solutions.

USING & APPLYING

PROBLEM SOLVING
◗ Decide how to use money to solve problems.
COMMUNICATION
◗ Invent simple ways of recording.

TALK ABOUT
◗ 'Could you use the number square to find out which numbers you have made so far?'
◗ 'What if you only used 3p stamps?'
◗ 'Are there any amounts that you don't think you will be able to make with these stamps?'

HERE'S THE MATHS
◗ This activity encourages flexibility in calculation, focusing on multiples of 3 and 5 and on addition. Children will find that it is not possible to make some small amounts – 1, 2, 4, 7 – but after that all are possible.

WHAT TO LOOK FOR
◗ Are the children familiar with all multiples of 3 and 5?
◗ Do they realise that they can be mixed in any proportion?

MORE HELP NEEDED
◗ If children are unable to think of a way of recording suggest that they divide the paper into sections like this:

Value	Coins	Stamps
11p	10p	
	1p	

◗ Children could concentrate on making amounts up to 20p.

FAIR SHARES
MATHS FOCUS – NUMBER KIT 3

Name _____

Stamps

PHOTOCOPIABLE

FAIR SHARES
MATHS FOCUS – NUMBER KIT 3

ENRICHMENT ACTIVITY

Grab it!

Key aims
◗ To develop the use of decimal notation.
◗ To give practice in using a calculator to add money.
◗ To develop the ability to interpret the calculator display in the context of money.

What you need
◗ a bank of coins, including some pound coins, in a bag or covered box
◗ calculators, including one with a large display if possible
◗ pencils

Organisation
◗ Ensure that you have all the resources ready to hand and that you have included pound coins.
◗ The children could help with organising the equipment.

The activity
◗ Show the children how to 'grab' a few coins from the box, then ask them how you could find out their total value.
◗ Encourage them to come up with a variety of methods and, if no-one suggests it, use the calculator.
◗ Demonstrate what happens when you enter an amount that is a multiple of 10, for example, £2.60, and add it to another amount, such as 70p. If the children have not tried this type of addition on the calculator before, let them have a few goes at entering and adding their own 'over a pound and ending in zero' numbers.
◗ Once they have understood the problems that can arise, make sure that amounts under a pound are entered as 'no pounds and so many pence'; explain that the decimal point separates the pounds from the pence and if it wasn't entered the calculator would treat the amount as pounds.
◗ Discuss the activity sheet and leave the children to work on the problem.

Extension idea
◗ Increase the number of £1 and 1p coins and remove all others. This will give the children more opportunity to practise using decimal notation, where zero is the place holder, as in £5.09 or £3.02.

USING & APPLYING

COMMUNICATION
◗ Develop the ability to work with others.

TALK ABOUT
◗ 'How will you enter this amount into the calculator?'
◗ 'Why must you do it like this?'
◗ Do you think that answer is likely to be right?'

HERE'S THE MATHS
◗ The recording of this activity demonstrates the children's understanding of zero as a place holder and decimal notation in money.

WHAT TO LOOK FOR
◗ Are the children recording each coin or adding them together?
◗ Are the children entering pence into the calculator correctly (for example, 0.70 rather than 70 for 70p)?
◗ Do they understand why they must do it like this?

Name _____

Grab it!

Take turns to take a handful of coins from the box.
Find out how much they are worth altogether by using your calculator.
Record your total in two ways:

My grabs

_____ or _____

                                                              _____ or _____

_____ or _____

                                                              _____ or _____

_____ or _____

                                                              _____ or _____

USING & APPLYING

PROBLEM SOLVING
- Show perseverance and overcome difficulties.

COMMUNICATION
- Read and write fractions.
- Show knowledge of the structure of the number system.

TALK ABOUT

- 'Can you see a pattern in the way these numbers grow?'
- 'Why did you put that fraction there?'
- 'What do you think will come next?'
- 'What do you think will come before zero?'

ENRICHMENT ACTIVITY

Fraction number lines

Key aims
- To develop understanding of how fractions are ordered within the number system.
- To use existing knowledge of fractions to build fraction number lines.

What you need
- 1 activity sheet for each child
- pencils and paper
- several sheets of scrap paper, halved
- a supply of coloured rods

The activity
- Lay out the scrap paper and remind the children that if a whole piece is cut into two equal parts, then both parts are halves.
- Show the children how to 'skip count' in halves: 'half a sheet, one sheet, one and a half sheets, two, two and a half…'
- Encourage the children to join in as soon as they can recognise the pattern.
- Start again, but this time count around the group, with each child saying the next fractional number in the sequence.
- Discuss the activity sheets with the children and leave them to work on them. Encourage them to fill in some numbers on the blank number lines, and then to challenge a friend to complete them.

Extension idea
- Ask the children to make their own fraction number lines on blank paper. They will have to measure out the divisions carefully but this will reinforce the fact that fractional steps on a line must be the same size, just as equal fractions of objects are of equal size.

FAIR SHARES

Name _____

Fraction number lines

Fill in the missing numbers on these fraction number lines.

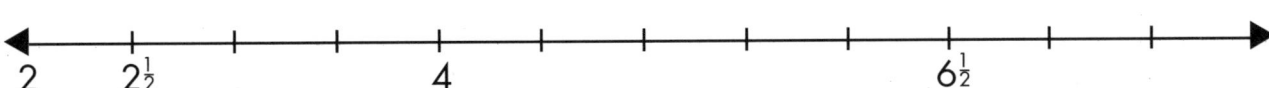

2   2½   4   6½

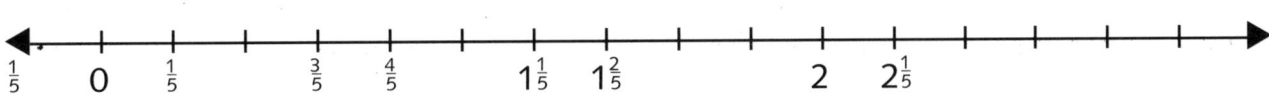

⅕   0   ⅕   ⅗   ⅘   1⅕ 1⅖   2   2⅕

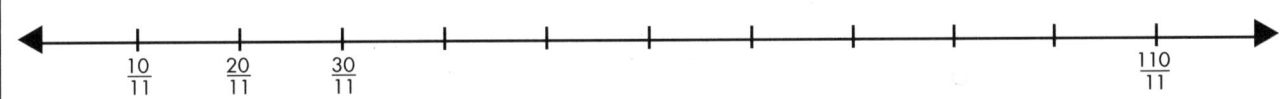

10/11 20/11 30/11   110/11

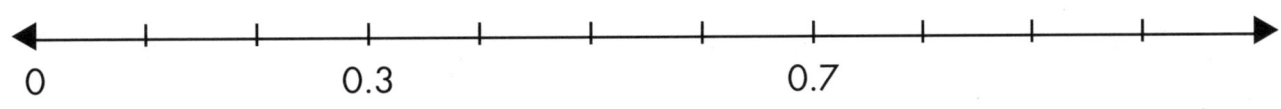

0   0.3   0.7

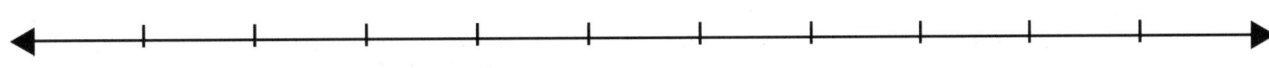

PHOTOCOPIABLE

USING & APPLYING

PROBLEM SOLVING
- Decide how to plan and organise a problem.
- Plan a suitable sequence of work for a set task.

TALK ABOUT

- 'Can you explain what you have done there?'
- 'What will the next shape you draw look like?'
- 'How will you start the next one?'
- 'Which is your favourite shape? Why?'

ENRICHMENT ACTIVITY

Design a decimal fraction

Key aims
- To provide experience of linking fractions and decimal fractions.
- To introduce the convention of recording using decimal notation.

What you need
- 1 grid sheet (page 47) per child
- 1 activity sheet between two
- colouring pencils

The activity
- Prepare a sheet of paper by folding it into tenths:

- Group the children around you.
- Show the children the folded paper and discuss the way that it has been folded.
- Ask them if they can identify any fractions – they may suggest halves, fifths or tenths. If they do not suggest tenths point this out.
- Cut out a piece representing two tenths of the whole:
- Tell the children that two tenths is written as $^2/_{10}$. Draw attention to the numerator, reminding them that it tells how many pieces of the whole the fraction represents.
- Explain that they are going to learn a new way to represent tenths called a **decimal**. Write 0.2 and explain that the decimal point separates the whole ones from the tenths. In this case there are no whole ones so a zero is used.
- Draw the children some more examples, then, when you judge that they are ready, give each pair an activity sheet and two sheets of grid paper (page 47).
- Discuss the task with the children to check they understand before leaving them to work independently.

Extension idea
- The children could work on designs in which they use decimal fractions greater than 1. This might involve colouring 11 or more triangles on the grid.

FAIR SHARES

Name _____

Design a decimal fraction

If you have a shape which has ten equal parts each part is $\frac{1}{10}$ of the whole.
If you colour four sections you have coloured four tenths of the shape.

You can write this as a decimal:

0.4

no units   four tenths

Design different 'wholes' divided into ten equal parts.
Colour each design in two colours or shade them with two patterns and label them as a decimal fraction and a fraction like this:

0.5 has spots $\frac{5}{10}$ has spots

0.5 has stars $\frac{5}{10}$ has stars

PHOTOCOPIABLE

ENRICHMENT ACTIVITY

Bank it!

Key aim
▶ To develop the ability to count out sums of money involving amounts over £1.

What you need
▶ 1 postermat game track (or the photocopiable version on page 48) and one activity sheet between two
▶ a bank of coins
▶ 1 dice for each pair of children
▶ 1 counter for each player

The activity
▶ Discuss the game with the children and make sure that they understand the rules.
▶ Check that they can count out amounts up to £3 and suggest that they try to make the sums from the smallest number of coins.
▶ Hand out the postermats and leave the children, in pairs, to play the game. If they are using the photocopiable version of the postermat point out that the yellow squares have been coloured black.

Extension ideas
▶ Use the same game track to practise making up amounts from a specific number of coins.
• Use two dice. The first one tells how many spaces to move forward, the second how many coins you may take from the bank.
• If the amount shown on the square can be made then take those coins.
• The winner is the player with the most money at the end of the game.

USING & APPLYING

PROBLEM SOLVING
▶ Check results (decide if the amount of coins counted out is correct).
LOGICAL REASONING
▶ Connect facts and ideas learned from working with small amounts of money to using larger amounts.

HERE'S THE MATHS
▶ This game encourages the practice of mental addition and subtraction of amounts of money.

WHAT TO LOOK FOR
▶ Can the children work out the amounts of money in their heads, or do they use the coins?

MORE HELP NEEDED
▶ Start with a smaller amount of money.
▶ Make sure that these are always enough coins for the addition.

Name _____

Bank it!

Take £3.00 in coins for each player from the bank, and a coloured counter.
Take turns to throw the dice.
Move your counter the number of squares shown by the dice.
If you land on a yellow square **take** the amount on the square from the bank.
If you land on any other colour square **pay** the amount on the square to the bank.
The player with the most money when you have both reached the end wins.

USING & APPLYING

COMMUNICATION
- Explain the work being done, including processes and difficulties.

LOGICAL REASONING
- Show the ability to reach conclusions by connecting facts and ideas from previous experience.

TALK ABOUT

- 'Which is your best journey so far?'
- 'Can you see another way to make the same amount of money?'
- 'How did you work out how much money you won?'
- 'How much more would you need to get to £1?'

HERE'S THE MATHS

- This activity offers further practice in adding amounts of money.

WHAT TO LOOK FOR

- How do the children carry out the calculations?

ENRICHMENT ACTIVITY

Money journeys

Key aims
- To give practice in totalling coins.
- To develop strategies in the context of a game.

What you need
- 1 activity sheet showing the game rules and recording chart and the Money journeys game board (postermat or page 48) between each pair of children
- dry-wipe markers
- pencils and paper
- a bank of money
- calculators

Organisation
- Ensure that there are sufficient postermat game boards for the children to have one between two – if not, take copies of the photocopiable version on page 48.

The activity
- Explain the activity to the children using the rules sheet.
- Tell them that you are going to take your marker for a walk to visit eight coins, building up your money total as you go.
- Ask them to suggest the steps of your journey as you go along, reminding them that you can only visit each coin once.
- When you have finished ask them to tell you how much your journey was worth. Some may need to collect coins to represent those on the board, others may calculate using paper and pencil, calculators or mentally.
- Ask for a volunteer to show a journey that would be worth more money.
- When you are sure that the children have understood how to play the game, and record their scores, let them play in pairs. Set a time limit, perhaps 10 minutes or a maximum number of moves, and talk to the children, when that limit has expired, about the journeys they have made.
- Ask them to compare their game board with another pair's.
- Best journeys can be recorded on a copy of page 48.

Extension ideas
- Encourage the children to generate questions which they can then try to answer, such as, 'which is the cheapest journey... the most expensive... the one that gives you a total nearest to £1'.
- Let the children make their own coin game board using drawn or cut-out coins.

Name _____

Money journeys

- You need a partner and a Money journeys game board between you.
- Take it in turns to draw a journey on your game board. Start at the edge, visit eight coins (or as many as you can in the time allowed) but do not go to a coin more than once.
- Work out what your journey was worth (with your partner's help) and record it on your side of the scoresheet.
- When the time limit is up find the total score for all your journeys.

Scoresheet

Name	Name
Total	Total

PHOTOCOPIABLE

Three in a line

$\frac{1}{2}$ of $\frac{1}{3}$ of

$\frac{1}{4}$ of $\frac{1}{5}$ of

6	4	2	24
10	14	26	32
30	16	9	20
18	13	15	12

6	7	3	2	8
4	$4\frac{1}{2}$	16	5	3
2	13	$6\frac{1}{2}$	10	15
$7\frac{1}{2}$	8	1	9	12

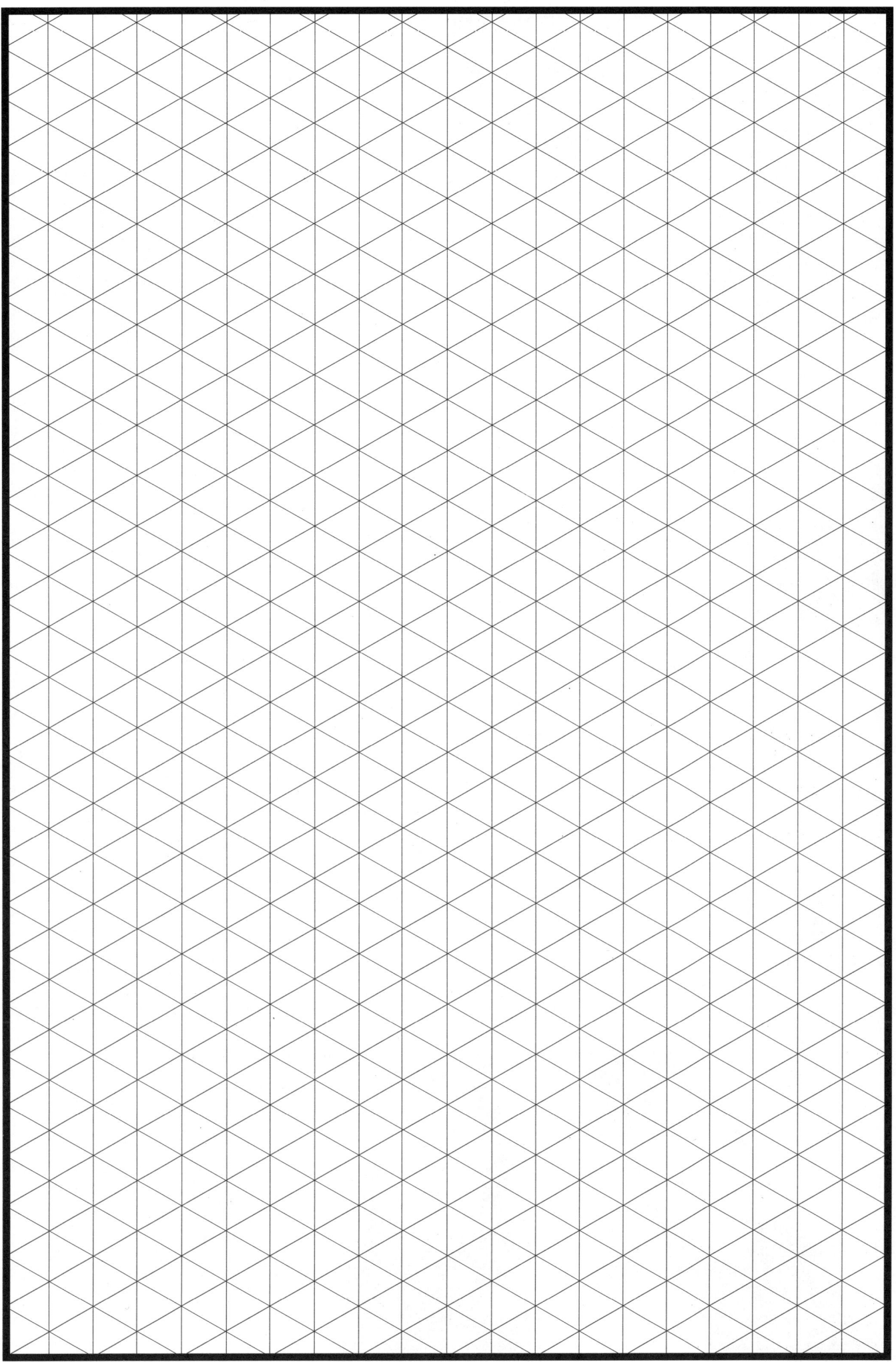

SEE PAGES 42 AND 44

| Start 1 | 2 | 3 | 4 | 5 | 6 |
| £1.02 | £0.37 | £0.54 | £1.63 | £0.98 | £0.76 |

7 £2.73
8 £0.09
9 £0.86
10 £1.01
11 £0.45
12 £0.38
13 £1.13
14 £0.02
15 £1.10
16 £2.60
17 £0.70
18 £1.15
19 £1.19
20 £0.83
21 £0.11
22 £1.17
23 £1.00
24 £1.10
25 £0.10

48 FAIR SHARES
MATHS FOCUS – NUMBER KIT 3

PHOTOCOPIABLE